The Great Court at the British Museum

The Deutsche Bibliothek holds
a record for this publication in the
Deutsche Nationalbibliografie;
detailed bibliographical data can
be found under http://dnb.ddb.de

Library of Congress Control
Number is available

©2011, Foster + Partners,
London, and Prestel Verlag,
Munich · London · New York

Prestel Verlag, A Member
of Verlagsgruppe Random
House GmbH

Prestel Verlag
Neumarkter Str. 28
81673 Munich
Germany
Tel   +49 (0)89 4136-0
Fax +49 (0)89 4136-2335
www.prestel.de

Prestel Publishing
900 Broadway, Suite 603
New York, NY 10003
USA
Tel   +1 (212) 995-2720
Fax +1 (212) 995-2733

Prestel Publishing Ltd
4 Bloomsbury Place
London
WC1A 2QA
UK
Tel +44 (020) 7323-5004
Fax +44 (020) 7636-8004
www.prestel.com

ISBN 978-3-7913-4590-1

The Great Court at the British Museum Foster + Partners

Norman Foster
Deyan Sudjic

PRESTEL
MUNICH · LONDON · NEW YORK

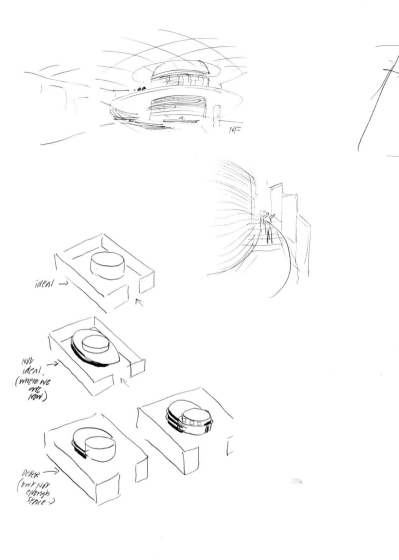

ideal →

not ideal (where we are now) →

better (but not enough space) →

Norman Foster's sketches explore the design of the Great Court and the arrangement of the new accommodation in relation to the drum of the Reading Room. One of the first issues to be addressed was the question of ramps versus stairs for access to the new levels.

Overleaf: An aerial view of the British Museum and the roof of the Great Court.

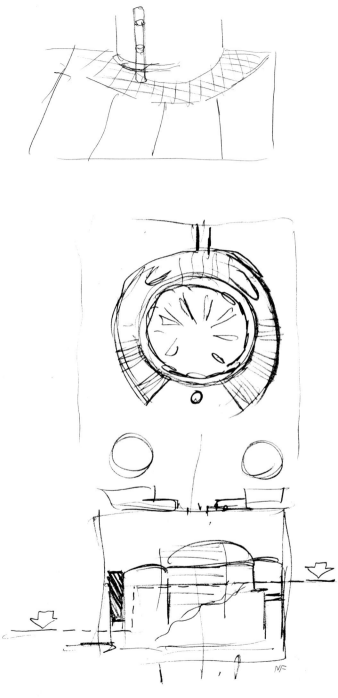

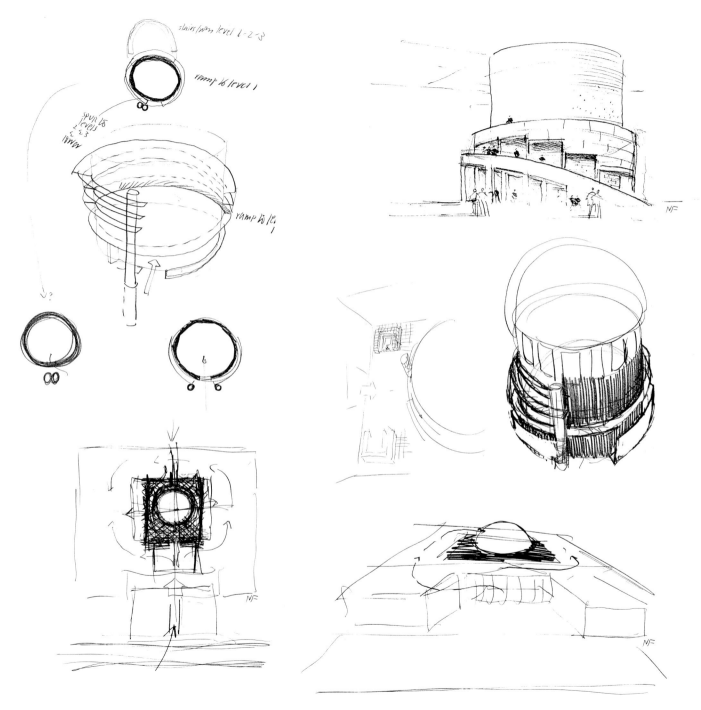

stairs/bars level 1-2-3

ramp to level 1

spur to levels 1 2 3

ramp to lev

Introduction Norman Foster

The courtyard that is now at the heart of the British Museum was one of London's long-lost spaces. In 1852, when Sir Robert Smirke's building was completed, the galleries were arranged around a fine quadrangle, open to the sky. However, within just five years, Sydney Smirke, who succeeded his brother as the museum's architect, had completely filled this fine space with the drum of the Reading Room and its associated bookstacks. Without the courtyard the museum lacked a central focus – it was like a city without a park. Our project was about its reinvention.

In terms of its number of visitors – approaching six million a year – the British Museum is one of the world's most popular cultural institutions, second only to the Louvre in Paris. That degree of popularity would put demands on any building. In the British Museum, which was designed in an age when 100,000 visitors a year were expected, it caused a critical level of congestion. Visitors had to push their way through one gallery to get to the next. The departure of the British Library from the museum to St Pancras presented the opportunity to address these problems and to transform the visitor experience as a whole.

By peeling away the unwanted structures around the Reading Room we were able to rediscover the historic courtyard and enclose it with a gossamer-like roof to create the Great Court. The project, however, extends far beyond this space. It comprises a series of interlinked elements, which form a complex, three-dimensional whole. In addition to the Great Court itself, we reinstated the museum's forecourt; restored the original decorative schemes in the Entrance Hall and the Reading Room; created a visitor centre for children in the vaults beneath the portico; and designed the Clore Education Centre and the Sainsbury African Galleries, both of which are entirely new and lie beneath the courtyard floor. The final piece, the Wellcome Trust Gallery for Ethnography, was completed in 2003.

One of my earliest drawings explored the way in which the Great Court lies on the cultural pedestrian route that runs through London like a leyline from the British Library in the north to Covent Garden, the river and the Southbank. I saw that we could create a new public route through the museum and, in doing so, achieve a better balance between the museum itself and the city as a whole.

It followed that the Great Court should offer an urban experience in microcosm. Unlike most museums, where the first thing you see is the gift shop, as you enter the Great Court from the south the Reading Room sits before you like a rotunda in a Renaissance *città ideale*, surrounded by the hustle and bustle of the museum. And just as in a traditional European city you might move from a confined passageway into a formal piazza, flooded with light, within the Great Court there are compressions and explosions of space. The irregular profile of the new elements around the Reading Room drum generates moments where you feel almost within touching distance of a carved capital or the framing of the roof. At other points the space soars above you. Again like a city, this variety of experiences encourages exploration. And it can be seen to work: the cafés are always crowded and sales in the bookshop have soared, so in turn there are commercial benefits for the museum.

A building on this scale – one that has evolved over a period of 150 years – is like a city in another sense, its fabric the product of different periods and styles. Along with the Royal Academy of Arts in London and the Reichstag in Berlin, the British Museum is one of a family of historical buildings in which we have made contemporary interventions. In each case the new reveals something fresh about the old. At the Royal Academy we can enjoy the dialogue between Burlington's Palladian villa and the Victorian galleries, which face each other across the newly inhabited light well. In the Reichstag we see history literally revealed in the Russian graffiti, masons' marks and the scars of war.

When I first visited the British Museum for this project the remnants of the courtyard were visible only from above; in fact few knew it existed at all. We have peeled back the layers of history to open it up once again. The Great Court is both a new organisational hub and the catalyst for the museum's reinvigoration.

The once virtually secret world of the Reading Room has also been opened up to the light. Historically, only scholars engaged in academic research had access to this extraordinary space. Now, as a new Library of World Culture it is open to the public for the first time and plays a central role as the museum's information centre. Here visitors can access a computer database that allows a virtual tour of the collections, or spend time in quiet study. The interior of the Reading Room dome has been restored to its original splendour, reinstating the azure, cream and gold decorative scheme that Sydney Smirke devised in 1857.

The Reading Room was originally only viewed from the inside; above the level of the bookstacks its external treatment was utilitarian brickwork. Now that the drum of the Reading Room has been revealed, it has been clad in limestone, which unites the free-standing structures visually with the Great Court's facades and the new floor; the masonry elements providing a foil to the lightness of the roof.

The glazed canopy that makes the activity of the Great Court possible fuses state-of-the-art engineering with economy of form. It is also sustainable environmentally, encouraging natural ventilation in the courtyard, while its glazing maximises transparency but minimises solar gain. The roof's triangulated geometry results from the challenge of spanning the irregular gap between the dome of the Reading Room and the courtyard facades. It is a unique form, sculpted to create large vaults with delicately thin members. Such a roof could not have been realised at any point in the museum's past; but it too has a history.

From our early collaborations with Buckminster Fuller – 'Bucky' as he was known affectionately – we have explored the potential of lightweight, transparent enclosures to liberate spatial possibilities; and like Bucky, we have always aimed to 'do the most with the least' and in the most elegant manner.

One such study, undertaken with Bucky in 1971, was the Climatroffice – a free-form dome within which the open floors enjoyed their own microclimate. Another antecedent of the Great Court, dating from

1979, is our project for a transport interchange and office complex in Hammersmith, which proposed a public space on the scale of Trafalgar Square. Enclosed by a translucent canopy and planted to evoke London's garden squares, this urban room would have been 'green' in more than one sense, forming a climatic buffer for the surrounding buildings, thereby reducing their energy needs. The idea of the sheltering 'umbrella' can also be found in the roof canopy of Stansted Airport, which allowed us to reinvent the airport, recasting the passenger concourse as a free-flowing, luminous space. At the epic scale of our later Beijing Airport the roof takes on the scale of an artificial sky.

Although there is an echo in the Great Court of Bucky's Manhattan dome, its urban roots lie historically in the nineteenth-century public arcades and galleries – such as Burlington Arcade in London, or the Galleria Vittorio Emanuele in Milan – that traditionally formed shortcuts through a city. Such spaces have been eroded over time, but we challenged ourselves to rediscover some of their lessons and to reapply them here in a contemporary manner. We also re-examined some of our own projects from the recent past, such as the piazza beneath the Commerzbank tower in Frankfurt. In common with all these spaces, within the museum the Great Court is both a route and a destination in its own right – a popular rendezvous for those who live and work in Bloomsbury.

The ability of a major cultural building to provide the catalyst for social and economic renewal in a community is demonstrated powerfully by our Carré d'Art in Nîmes, which brought a change of fortune for an entire urban quarter. The outdoor café life that thrives there also reflects a benign southern climate. In the Great Court the roof creates a microclimate that similarly invites a leisurely approach to life. To promenade there, to buy a book or a magazine and read it over a coffee is to enjoy an experience unlike that to be found in any other London museum.

The Great Court can also be understood in the context of our central London masterplan, in which we made detailed proposals for the environmental improvement of Trafalgar Square, Parliament Square, Whitehall and its environs. The emphasis there was on improving pedestrian access and enhancing the setting of some of the capital's most important historic buildings and monuments.

There are interesting parallels between Trafalgar Square and the British Museum as they were and as they have been reinvented. In both cases, people were once forced to circulate around the edges of an underused or inaccessible space. In the square it was the narrow pavement next to the traffic; in the museum it was through the perimeter galleries. The design solutions in each case opened up a new heart, with the possibility of diagonal movement and urban shortcuts.

When we first came to the project, the museum's forecourt was used as a staff car park, which utterly compromised the entrance to one of the world's great institutions. By going back to its historical roots, we saw an opportunity to return a major urban space to London. We banished the cars, reinstated the stone paving and formal lawns according to Robert Smirke's geometry and integrated seating into new stone enclosures. Today the forecourt provides a dignified setting for the museum and offers visitors a herald of the Great Court.

One of Bucky's ambitions for his Manhattan dome was that it should promote fresh means of experiencing the city. Beneath its own glass sky the Great Court has created new ways of accessing and enjoying the museum's collections and pioneered patterns of social use hitherto unknown within this or any other museum. The Great Court is a new kind of civic space – a cultural piazza – which people are invited to use and enjoy from early in the morning to late at night. In a crowded city and a busy museum it is an oasis.

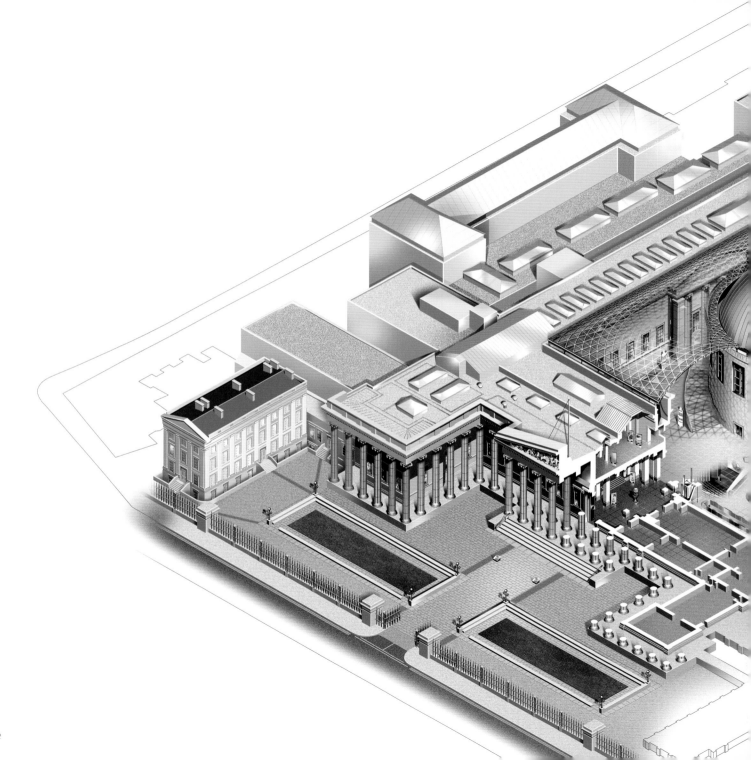

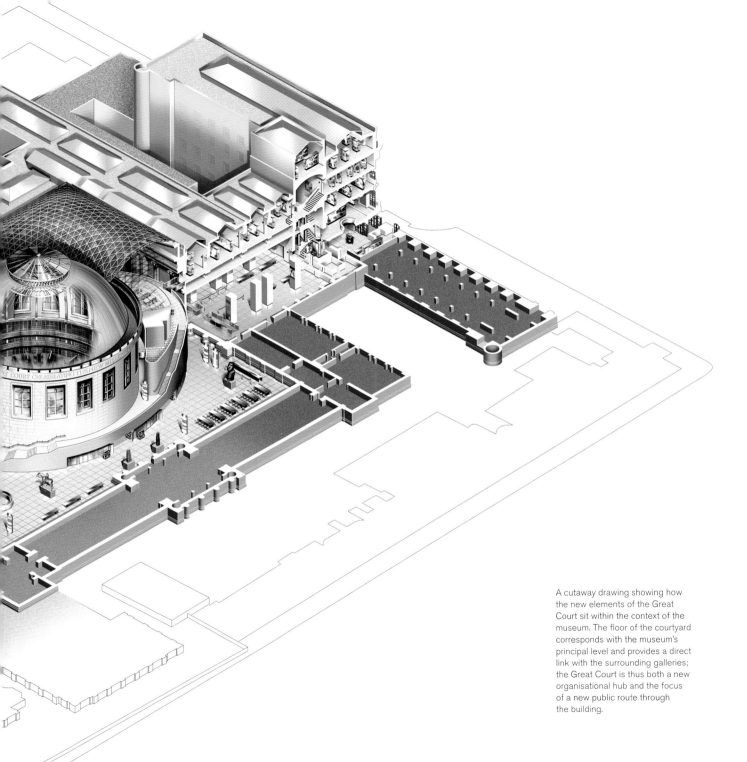

A cutaway drawing showing how the new elements of the Great Court sit within the context of the museum. The floor of the courtyard corresponds with the museum's principal level and provides a direct link with the surrounding galleries; the Great Court is thus both a new organisational hub and the focus of a new public route through the building.

13

Rediscovering the Great Court Deyan Sudjic

The Great Court at the British Museum is the product of the work of no fewer than three architects, along with a nineteenth-century librarian and the museum's last twentieth-century director. Only the first of them, Sir Robert Smirke, who defined its shape and proportions, had an entirely free hand. And even he had to create a plan that allowed the museum to be built in gradual stages around Montagu House, its original home, which in turn was demolished equally slowly. At its heart was a great courtyard that Smirke saw as a fitting consummation of the expectations aroused by the heroic scale of the Ionic entrance front.

Sydney Smirke, egged on by Antonio Panizzi, the brilliant Italian exile who made the museum's library one of the greatest of its kind in the world, obliterated his elder brother's courtyard by filling it with the round Reading Room. What had been an open space on the scale of Hanover Square became a great domed interior, reserved for scholars, with a hinterland of utilitarian bookstacks which lapped like flotsam at the edges of the library and the courtyard that contained it.

The third architect is Norman Foster, who together with his partner Spencer de Grey, transformed the centre of the museum for a second time – pulling off the difficult feat of reconciling his predecessors' visions one with the other, allowing both courtyard and Reading Room to coexist. Foster's work is of a scale and complexity that makes it far more than an extension or a simple addition. It is at the very heart of the museum, and amounts to a fundamental re-examination not just of its architecture but of the very nature of one of Britain's most important cultural institutions.

Foster was moved by the memory of the lost courtyard and its part in Sir Robert Smirke's original design. As he observes in his introduction to this book, 'Without this space the Museum lacked a central focus – it was like a city without a park. Our project is about its reinvention'.

From its creation more than 250 years ago, the British Museum has gone through a pattern of expansion and contraction that could almost be seen as a detailed working model of the 'Big Bang' theory of the creation of the universe, which the museum might well have in one of its countless glass cabinets. In the beginning there was nothing. Nobody believed in building a free museum for the instruction and gratification of the public, as the Act of Parliament establishing the British Museum specified. Then suddenly and apparently without warning floating clouds of dust fused to make the universe in a single creative explosion.

1754

1852

1857

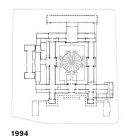

1994

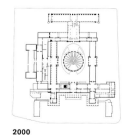

2000

Left: An idealised view of the British Museum's courtyard, dating from the mid-nineteenth century; although planned as a garden, the public was never granted access to the space.

Opposite: A sequence of plans showing the development of the British Museum, from its foundation in Montagu House in 1753 to the completion of the Great Court in 2000. The round Reading Room was built in 1857, only five years after the courtyard itself had been completed.

Above: The south front of the British Museum, as depicted in 1848.

Above: The Reading Room, photographed in 1925. JJ Burnet's white and gold colour scheme of 1907 had been darkened to 'elephant grey' by the polluted London air.

Right: A view of the austere brick drum of the Reading Room, circa 1943.

The Big Bang in this case is represented by the moment in 1753 when Parliament passed the Act accepting the bequest of a sprawling collection built up by Sir Hans Sloane. Sloane had been a highly successful physician, serving three successive sovereigns, Queen Anne, George I and George II. He had filled his house in Bloomsbury Place, and the one next door, which he bought to contain ever-growing numbers of exotic plants, fruits, coral, mineral stones, ferns, shells, fossils, coins, medals, Classical and medieval antiquities and books. In 1742 he removed both himself and his collection to much larger premises in Chelsea. Sloane was a significant European figure, Voltaire visited him, and when Handel came for tea, he outraged his host by carelessly placing a plate of buttered muffins on one of Sloane's rare manuscripts.

Sloane's collection was joined with that of Sir Robert Cotton, another extraordinary collector who had specialised in books and manuscripts. Chief among the prizes in Cotton's library were the Lindisfarne Gospel, the Anglo-Saxon Chronicle and the Magna Carta. These private collections were acquired by the state and combined to make the core of the British Museum. A lottery was authorised by Parliament to fund the housing of the collection, just as the National Lottery would later part-fund the creation of the Great Court.

Montagu House, a mansion on the site of the present museum, originally built in 1675, was acquired to house the collections, and so for the first seventy-five years of its existence, the British Museum showed its collections in the fundamentally domestic setting of a great house. While the museum was open to the public, free of charge, it was, in the early nineteenth century a very different place from its contemporary incarnation, with visitors numbered in thousands rather than millions. There was very little artificial light and little attempt at explanation or display techniques. Visitors needed an admission ticket, which might take six months to acquire. Unless they were known to museum staff, curious scholars and early tourists alike were marched around Montagu House by guides – one visitor described them as 'ciceroni' – who would rush them through as fast as possible, weaving through the cluster of stuffed giraffes on the main staircase, through the galleries of coins and books, until they could usher them back out into the street.

The biggest physical change in the museum's history was prompted by the acquisition of its most famous exhibit, the Elgin Marbles, which were accepted by the British government in 1816. So crowded and chaotic had the museum become that the marbles had to be accommodated in a temporary shed. With the other archaeological additions to the collection, the trustees began to see that expanding Montagu House was no longer a viable strategy. A new building was inevitable. Sir Robert Smirke, one of the architects retained by the government, was asked to design a suitable structure in 1823. It was the first step in a Europe-wide explosion of museum building.

Leo von Klenze began work on the Glyptothek, in Munich, in 1816; Karl Friedrich Schinkel designed Berlin's Altes Museum in 1823, though building did not start until 1825. But it was the British Museum, as much as any of the period, that established the Classical temple as the archetype for future generations of museums. And given the fact that its greatest treasures were taken from the Parthenon, how could it not have taken its inspiration from that building's austere Classicism?

Yet despite the impression of permanence evoked by the Classical language of Smirke's building, his proposals took shape gradually. He devised a plan that allowed the museum to be built in phases around Montagu House, which in turn was demolished equally slowly. Without ever being closed entirely to visitors the museum was thirty years in the building; and within seven years of its completion the courtyard had been colonised by the round Reading Room.

Above: As part of their preliminary research for the project, the team documented the congestion that was unfortunately an occupational hazard of a visit to the museum.

By its very nature, the British Museum has never been a static institution: throughout its history, it has continually changed shape and form, despite acquiring the thick crust of tradition that gives the illusion of conservatism. Foster's notion of 'reinvention' therefore seems entirely appropriate. It is also a complex organism with its own traditions, prejudices and inevitable conflicts. It grew from disparate private collections to become the most significant repository of archaeological remains in the world. Then it metamorphosed once again to become one of the world's greatest libraries: the Reading Room is the place from which figures such as Mahatma Gandhi and Karl Marx set out to change the course of history.

And yet at the same time the museum has had within it the seeds of its own eventual destruction. The more it has excelled at amassing a general collection; the greater has been the pressure for it to specialise. Continual expansion has inevitably led to subsequent eruptions. From being an attempt at a universal collection of everything, growth inevitably resulted in increasing specialisation. And most of those specialised collections have spun out of the original institution. The British Museum gave up its pictures to establish the National Gallery in 1828, a mere twelve years after it had acquired the Elgin Marbles. Its plant

specimens, geological collections, stuffed birds and dinosaurs went to create the Natural History Museum in 1880. The gaps were filled by the massive expansion of the museum's collections of books and documents.

For a while it seemed that Panizzi, who created what eventually became the British Library, would swallow the museum whole. 'Paris must be surpassed' he would urge his assistants, as the British Museum rapidly overtook the Bibliothèque Nationale in size and importance, its collection of books and documents doubling and redoubling every ten years. For 150 years the Reading Room was one of the sacred sites of international scholarship. With its vast cast-iron skeleton it was also a spectacular demonstration of advanced nineteenth-century building technology. But its splendour concealed the cluttered squalor of the gradual accretion of bookstacks, offices and ancillary spaces that filled the courtyard. Finally, in 1998, after thirty years of plans and counter plans, the British Library itself moved out.

In the run up to the library's departure to Colin St John Wilson's new home for it next to St Pancras Station, the British Museum's director, Robert Anderson, began to think seriously about the implications of tearing such a hefty chunk out of the heart of the building. Historically most of the strategic

planning effort had been devoted, unsuccessfully,
to exploring ways of expanding the museum and
the British Library on its existing site further into
Bloomsbury. In the 1960s Sir Leslie Martin and Sir
Colin St John Wilson had proposed a scheme that
would have cleared a huge swathe of Georgian
Bloomsbury, as far as Hawksmoor's church on High
Holborn, carving out an open piazza with the library on
one side, creating a fine setting for the approach to the
museum. However, that plan was resisted by the newly
powerful conservationist lobby. Wilson subsequently
drew up a more modest scheme to squeeze the library
into a reduced site, which would still have required
an unacceptable amount of demolition, and also
met with resistance.

With the library's departure, there was a realisation
that the question of what to do with the space it
released could be as problematic as plans to
accommodate it had been in the past. The director
and the trustees had spent considerable time thinking
about how the space could be used. They wanted to
bring the ethnographic collections back to Bloomsbury
from the satellite Museum of Mankind, which had
been established to accommodate them in 1970, at
Burlington House behind the Royal Academy. The
museum also needed facilities for schoolchildren

and for lectures, it needed storage space, and
somewhere for all the shops and restaurants and
cafés that are now an integral part of the contemporary
museum experience. The Reading Room itself was
to be sacrosanct, but it also needed a new purpose.
It could not simply be embalmed: a witness to a
glorious but now vanished past.

In 1993 Anderson and the Museum trustees
launched an international architectural competition
(which attracted entries from 132 architects from
around the world) to find a way to deal with the empty
shell of the library, and the mess that encircled it. A
month later in December 1993, a shortlist of twenty-
two architects was selected. In March 1994 the
Museum invited three practices – Arup Associates,
Rick Mather and Foster + Partners – to go forward
to a second stage of the competition. Each was asked
to address a number of issues raised by their initial
submissions. In July 1994 Foster was declared winner.
From that point the project began to evolve in a
dialogue between architect and client. The Museum
appointed its head of administration, Chris Jones, as
the project sponsor and established a client committee,
led by the chairman of the trustees Graham Greene.
Robert Anderson and the museum's managing director
Suzanna Taverne also played key roles.

Left and above: Two views of the
1:200-scale sectional model, with
and without the courtyard roof,
presented at the second stage of
the competition in March 1994.

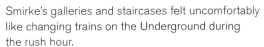

Right: A concept model showing new patterns of circulation created through the museum and access from the Great Court into the adjacent galleries.

The competition brief comprised a wish list of new amenities that any modern cultural institution would look for. But the key issue to deal with was one specific to the museum and its architectural history – that of space. It was apparent that the building itself, despite the splendour of its entrance front, had lost the clarity of Smirke's original plan. And with almost as many visitors annually as the Louvre in Paris, and more than the Metropolitan Museum of Art in New York, the museum had reached a level of popularity that was putting uncomfortably severe demands on the building and threatening to overwhelm it. Spencer de Grey recalls making his first reconnaissance visit to the museum for the competition and coming away with the abiding impression of how overcrowded it was.

Over time the museum had grown from a primarily academic, scholarly institution into a vast social magnet. Smirke had envisaged 100,000 visitors a year, but by the mid-1990s the museum was attracting more than that number each week, approaching six million visitors annually. Without the courtyard the museum galleries functioned like corridors, choked with visitors who were forced to use them as a circulation route to reach one part of the building from another. And there was nothing to provide a sense of orientation to tell you which part of the museum you were in. Negotiating

Smirke's galleries and staircases felt uncomfortably like changing trains on the Underground during the rush hour.

Though the competition brief had a set of highly specific requirements, it was also open to interpretation. 'The museum was looking for a story', says de Grey. And evidently he and Foster were able to create the kind of big-picture narrative that the museum wanted to hear. In essence, Foster's project is about orienting the visitor and giving the museum room to breathe. The departure of the British Library left a physical void at the very centre of the museum, a space which Foster's Great Court fills paradoxically by not filling, but creating instead one of London's greatest new urban spaces. This new 'cultural piazza' forms part of what Foster conceives as a new pedestrian route that links Bloomsbury with the Thames – a route that takes in the restored museum forecourt. Under Foster's direction this space was cleared of cars and repaved, and seating was integrated into new stone enclosures surrounding the reinstated turf.

At the time, it offered a taste of what Foster's vision of the partially pedestrianised Trafalgar Square would be like. 'We saw that we could create a new public route through the building, and in doing so, achieve a

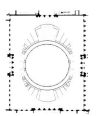

A plan of the Great Court at education centre level, as proposed at the second stage of the competition; this accommodation would subsequently be placed below the courtyard.

better balance between the museum as an entity and the city as a larger whole', recalls Foster.

Foster won the competition with a design that was much denser than the scheme he would finally build. There was a lightweight roof over the courtyard and there was circulation space within it. But the Reading Room would have been sheathed in an elliptical structure housing accommodation on two levels to both the north and south, which would have come to within 7 metres of the South Portico. The new accommodation was accessed by a stepped ramp that wound around the drum of the Reading Room. Below the main level of the Great Court was space for temporary exhibitions together with the considerable amount of storage suggested in the brief. In this configuration, the Great Court would not have had the same sense of space that it has now, and would have been the poorer for it. It was only once the project was under way that its full potential to do more than deal with the mundane round of museum housekeeping and accommodate the husk of the Reading Room became apparent.

In parallel with the dialogue between architect and client about the Great Court, a wider strategic discussion about the overall masterplan for the museum was taking place. This highlighted the fact

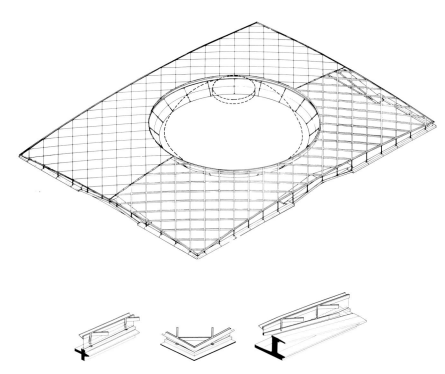

Above: A cutaway drawing and details of the roof structure as first envisaged; the ETFE 'pillows' were to be suspended in a steel frame with a square grid.

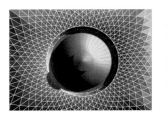

that certain elements of the competition brief could be reduced in size or relocated to other sites. By early 1995 the Foster team had developed the scheme. Retail accommodation was located under the ellipse to the south of the Reading Room. Educational facilities were positioned below the courtyard level to the south, with new African Galleries balancing them to the north – a move made possible by the museum's decision to relocate storage to a new Study Centre, planned in an old Post Office building at the other end of Museum Street. At this stage an elliptical structure was still wrapped around the outside of the Reading Room on two levels, although the ramp was now on the outer edge of the new accommodation.

By the autumn of 1995, the design had evolved still further. The accommodation that had formed the southern half of the ellipse was removed and replaced by a double staircase leading to two new levels, which were concentrated to the north. For the first time a major volume was created in the Great Court, linked spatially to the museum's main entrance. Instead of three bridge links to the upper-level galleries, there was now only one. A bookshop and the Sir Joseph Hotung Gallery were contained in a tiered stack of floors within what was now an ovoid structure to the north of the Reading Room. Accessed via a

symmetrical pair of staircases, which embraced the drum of the Reading Room, this 'bustle' culminated in a restaurant terrace level close to the pediment of the North Portico. The chief effect of these changes was to allow the Reading Room to be read as a discrete element in space, rather than as an integral part of a new building.

The final scheme takes a strategic view of the museum that extends far beyond the limits of the Great Court. Rather than being focused on a single space it is conceived as a sequence of eight interlinked elements: the forecourt has been freed from cars, and civilised with stone and gravel; the entrance hall has been restored; the Reading Room has been refurbished and opened to the public for the first time; the creation of the Clore Education Centre allows the museum to stage conferences and seminars on an international scale; the Ford Young Visitors Centre provides much-needed amenities for the 1,500 schoolchildren that visit the museum daily; there are the new Sainsbury African Galleries; and finally the transformation of the old North Library into the Wellcome Trust Gallery, completed in 2003, which has created more space for ethnographic displays and established a direct route through the museum from north to south.

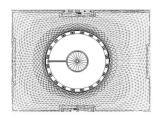

Above: A view of the 1:200-scale
sectional model of the scheme as
submitted for planning approval
in December 1995; although
the precise detail of the roof
canopy would continue to be
refined, all the major elements
of the scheme were in place.

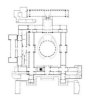  

The Great Court is clearly far more than a 'restoration' or an extension. It is the creation of something powerfully, distinctively new. Certainly it is one of the most challenging commissions of Foster's career, and perhaps a defining one. It mixes architecture and urban design, and it confronts the historical language of Classicism with elegant, computer-aided structural design, providing a level of geometric analysis that would never previously have been available. In this sense the spectacular glazed canopy that floats high above the floor of the Great Court has a shape that could not have existed at any other period, demonstrating engineering skills at the limits of contemporary understanding.

In presenting the project – and the precedents for the roof – Foster places it in a line of development for the practice that springs from his unbuilt Hammersmith Centre of 1977-1979. That project was an attempt to create an urban space with some of the qualities of two of Foster's enduring historical inspirations: Milan's Galleria Vittorio Emanuele and Joseph Paxton's Crystal Palace. He also refers to the lessons both technical and spatial that he gained from working with Buckminster Fuller; as Foster describes the roof structure, 'its geometry results from the challenge of spanning the irregular gap between the dome of the reading room and the courtyard facades – of doing the most with the least'.

The roof as realised is very different from the canopy of inflated ETFE (ethylene tetrafluoroethylene) 'pillows' that Foster investigated during the competition and for some time afterwards. This would have consisted of two layers of a translucent plastic foil filled with air, and supported on a regular diagonal grid, 4.3 metres square. As a material ETFE had some benefits over glass, chief among them being its availability in much larger sheets. The system also had excellent thermal characteristics because of the air trapped in the pillows; and the pillows could have been constructed with interlayers to block ultraviolet radiation.

However, closer study revealed that if it was configured in this way the roof would have been so light that it would have needed a heavy steel restraining structure to prevent it lifting off in strong winds. And although this system would have required fewer structural members than one using glass, they would have had to be much thicker to provide the necessary weight. Although the pillow solution was technically feasible, after careful deliberation Foster concluded that it was not appropriate for the Classical character of the courtyard. Square ETFE panels would

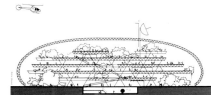

not have sat comfortably with the circular geometry of the drum and the rectangular courtyard; and the use of glass would allow a less visually intrusive structure.

The roof covers an area measuring 110 by 70 metres, and spans lengths varying from 14 metres, where the Reading Room is closest to the courtyard's facades, to 40 metres at the corners of the courtyard. The structure as finally realised is the product of sophisticated analysis, carried out in collaboration with engineers Buro Happold, with advice from Chris Williams, a mathematician at Bath University. The geometrical problems it presented were complicated by the fact that the Reading Room is located eccentrically in the courtyard, 5 metres closer to the north facade. And it had to be vaulted in order to clear the porticoes at the centre of each facade, but be shallow enough to minimise its visual impact from the surrounding streets. As a result no two of the roof's triangular glass panels are identical.

The roof's geometry is generated from a grid of radial elements that span between the circle of the Reading Room and the rectangle of the courtyard. These are interconnected by two opposing spirals, which allow the roof to work as a shell structure. Initially, the triangular openings were much bigger than they appear in the final design and they generated

irregular residual shapes around the perimeter, at the junction with the Reading Room and the courtyard walls. And at one point in its development, the roof comprised more than 10,000 triangular panels, compared with the 3,312 that make up the final design. Because the drum of the Reading Room is not at the centre of a single radiating pattern, the geometry gives the appearance of being non-linear, setting up multiple optical effects that suggest it is closer to the kind of elegant space container envisaged by Buckminster Fuller than to an architectural dome.

The amount of steelwork employed has been minimised by integrating the main structural elements with the fixings and support for the glass. Many different solutions were investigated before the design team arrived at the final integrated structural and glazing system, which employs rectangular hollow steel sections. In answer to the question that Buckminster Fuller would certainly have asked, the roof weighs almost 800 tonnes – roughly the same as the new cupola of the Reichstag. A very high grade of steel was used, one more typically used for marine or petrochemical applications. The steel lattice structure consists of 5,162 individual steel box beams that intersect at 1,826 unique structural six-way nodes – totalling some 11 kilometres of steelwork. Each

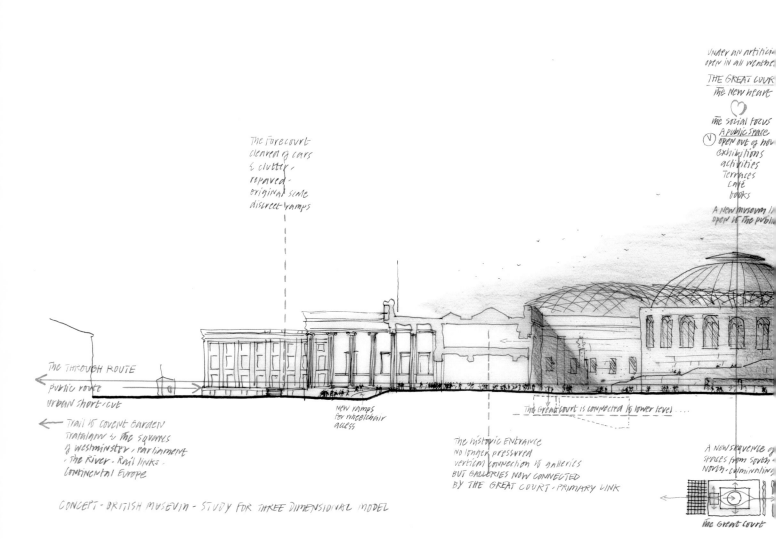

The Forecourt
cleared of cars
& clutter,
repaved·
original scale
discreet ramps

Under an artificial
open in all weather

THE GREAT COURT
The New heart

♡

The social focus
A public space
open out of new
exhibitions
activities
Terraces
café
books

A New museum
open to the public

The THROUGH ROUTE

Public route

Urban short-cut

Trail to Covent Garden
Trafalgar & the squares
of Westminster · Parliament
· The River · Rail links ·
Continental Europe

New ramps
for wheelchair
access

The historic Entrance
no longer preserved
vertical connection of galleries
BUT GALLERIES NOW CONNECTED
BY THE GREAT COURT · PRIMARY LINK

The Great court is connected to lower level

A New sequence of
spaces from south
North · culminating

The Great court

CONCEPT · BRITISH MUSEUM · STUDY FOR THREE DIMENSIONAL MODEL

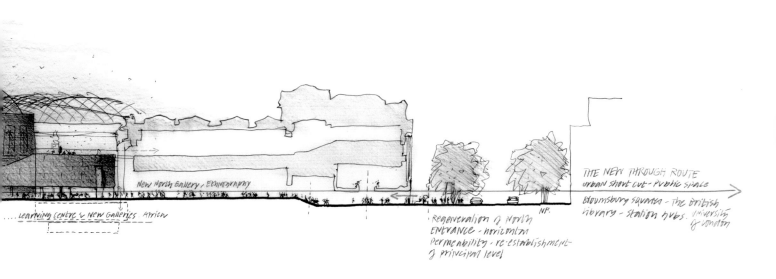

... Learning centre & New Galleries. Africa

New North Gallery / Ethnography

Regeneration of North ENTRANCE - horizontal permeability · re-establishment of principal level

NF.

THE NEW THROUGH ROUTE
urban short cut - public space

Bloomsbury square - the British library - station hubs. University of London

Norman Foster's cross-section through the Great Court provides a vivid illustration of the way in which the courtyard forms the focus of a new spatial sequence within the museum and its wider role as a social and cultural piazza within the city.

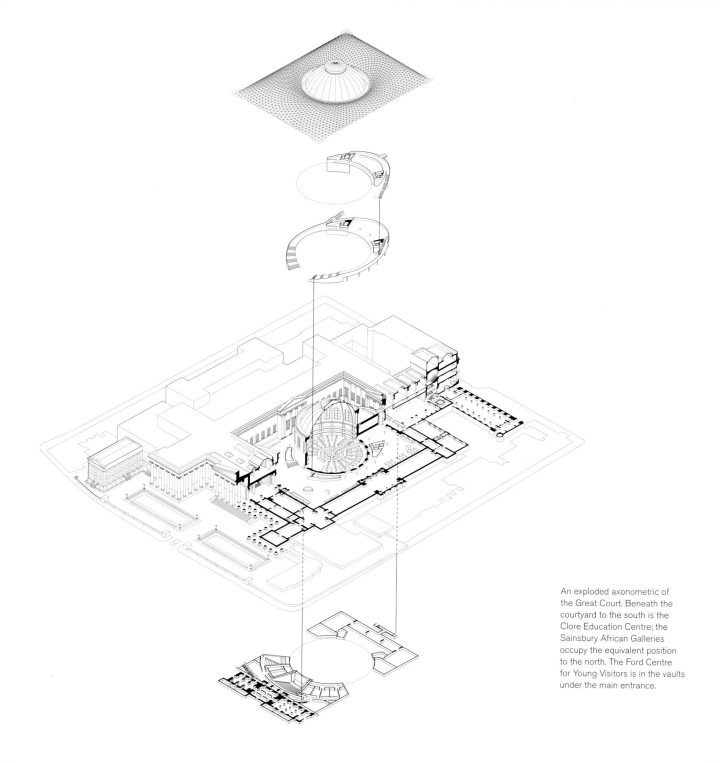

An exploded axonometric of the Great Court. Beneath the courtyard to the south is the Clore Education Centre; the Sainsbury African Galleries occupy the equivalent position to the north. The Ford Centre for Young Visitors is in the vaults under the main entrance.

1994

2000

node point in this complex grid had a theoretical position in space and the roof was constructed to within an accuracy of plus or minus 3mm for each and every node position – an error of just 0.015 per cent, which is astonishingly accurate for the modern building industry.

Construction began in 1997 and took thirty-three months to complete. Demolition alone took nine months with everything having to be lifted in or out by one of two cranes, the larger of which had a 75-metre jib. As the quadrant bookstacks gradually came down the courtyard facades were uncovered for the first time in more than 140 years, revealing the extensive damage inflicted to the columns of the east, west and north porticoes by construction work in the 1850s.

Before excavation could start it was necessary to stabilise parts of the Reading Room and the courtyard facades. Using a process called jet grouting, concrete was injected at high pressure beneath the existing structures to form new foundations. This was a finely balanced operation, which required that the Reading Room's structure be monitored constantly to ensure that no adverse stresses were placed upon it. With the Reading Room structure and Smirke facades stabilised, excavation works could begin. This process was complicated by the fact that the lowest levels

were below the water table and therefore needed to be drained continually.

As a preliminary to building the roof, the Great Court was enclosed by a temporary construction deck, creating as Spencer de Grey recalls, 'a subterranean world of scaffold poles, dimly lit construction materials and ubiquitous masonry dust.' Because the only access to the site was by means of the two cranes that towered over the museum there were inevitable restrictions on the size of components that could be used to construct the roof. In the months before the erection of the roof began, thousands of steel elements had been manufactured in Vienna by Waagner Biro (the same company that built the Reichstag's dome) and shipped to Derby where they were assembled into a series of ladder-like sections. These were then welded together on site to form the main structural grid. Over a period of six months these elements were craned daily on to the site; de Grey remembers that 'the construction deck became a vast sorting office with hundreds of steel elements carefully coded and stored in groups ready for erection on to temporary props.'

The assembly process was further complicated by the fact that the structure had to be built higher than its projected profile in order to allow it to settle as the

Above: Before and after views of the museum's courtyard, photographed in 1994 and 2000 respectively, looking towards the drum of the round Reading Room; the transformation is dramatic.

Right: Before and after views of the courtyard, looking towards the East Portico; the jumble of bookstacks and temporary buildings has been swept away and the space liberated.

1994

2000

glazing was installed. The glass panels were positioned in a prearranged sequence to ensure that the roof deflected in accordance with the engineers' own mathematical models. By the late spring of 2000 the majority of the glass had been installed, which meant that the temporary scaffolding could be removed. As the roof was gradually 'de-propped', and became self-supporting, the structure dropped 150mm and spread some 90mm laterally on its sliding bearings, precisely as predicted.

At its junction with the Reading Room the roof is supported on a ring of twenty slender tubular steel columns, which align with the existing building's cast-iron frame. These columns are concealed behind the Reading Room's stone cladding, which also provides space for vertical services risers containing rainwater pipes and ventilation ducts. The roof is prevented from spreading laterally at this point by a reinforced concrete 'snow gallery', which replaces the brick-arched structure that originally ringed the Reading Room dome to break the fall of heavy loads of snow from the roof. This structure acts as a stiffening diaphragm, balancing the thrusts from opposite sides of the roof, and is supported on sliding bearings, which allow the ring beam to float above the Reading Room's cast-iron frame.

At the perimeter of the courtyard the roof rests on Smirke's load-bearing masonry walls, connected by means of short steel columns to a new reinforced-concrete parapet beam. To avoid applying lateral loads to the existing structure, the roof is supported on sliding bearings, which allow it to flex in response to changes in temperature or the weight of snow and to transfer the loads vertically. At the four corners of the roof – where large forces are generated – the structure is stiffened by tension cables.

The roof is also designed with climate control in mind. The glazing system allows daylight to illuminate the courtyard and to enter the Reading Room and, in very controlled quantities, the surrounding galleries. In order to reduce solar heat gain the tinted glass panels are screen-printed with reflective ceramic dots over 56 per cent of their surface – a technique known as 'fritting'. Together with the roof's structure, the frits limit light penetration to only 30 per cent of the roof area and prevent 75 per cent of the sun's heat – as infrared radiation – from entering the courtyard.

Natural ventilation is provided in the Great Court by high-level louvres positioned around the edge of the roof (in winter these can be used to heat the incoming air). These louvres work in unison with a direct fresh-air feed to louvres at floor-level, which allow internal heat

Above left: Located below the Great Court, to the south of the Reading Room, the Clore Education Centre contains two auditoria and five seminar rooms, all linked by a grand curved foyer.

Above right: The larger auditorium can seat 320, the smaller 150 people. This new facility fulfils the needs of the museum's expanding education programme and allows it to stage conferences and seminars on an international scale.

Above: The Ford Centre for
Young Visitors provides facilities
for the 1,500 schoolchildren
that visit the museum daily. It
is situated at the level of the
original courtyard garden in
the Victorian vaults beneath
the entrance hall.

Right: The rebuilt South Portico follows the spirit of Smirke's original, which was demolished in 1877 to allow the enlargement of the Front Hall. However, it stands further forward in the courtyard than the original in order to accommodate new lifts.

gains to be vented through a natural stack effect. The incoming air is filtered in primary plant rooms located in the museum's basement. Heating comes from an underfloor system that relies on pipes embedded in the screed. The same pipework can be fed from the chilled water system, allowing the temperature in the Great Court to be maintained between 18°C in winter and 25°C in summer. The intention is not to climate control the entire volume, just the lower zone occupied by people. In the remainder of the new spaces full air conditioning is supplied via secondary plant rooms located beneath the courtyard.

As completed the Great Court is one of the most striking new architectural experiences in London, without actually being a building in its own right. Foster has deftly drained the courtyard of debris, to rediscover the ghost of the outdoor space that Sir Robert Smirke intended. Like an archaeologist, Foster reveals what was once there, but cannot recreate the space lost by the installation of a giant Victorian cuckoo in a chaste Ionic nest. He allows both to coexist by turning negative into positive space, almost in the manner of one of Rachel Whiteread's cast concrete sculptures. The space appears to takes its character from its surroundings but is anything but passive. It is an indoor space, but only just. Under the extraordinary glass

roof it is possible to watch the clouds glide by and to see the sun track across the stone floor.

This is far from Foster's first attempt to address a highly charged historical context. At the Royal Academy's Sackler Galleries, completed in 1991, there was also a play between Classical context and steel-and-glass insertions, as well as the unlocking of previously lost space. With the Carré d'Art in Nîmes (1984-1993) Foster had to work with one of France's finest surviving Roman monuments; and in Berlin retaining the Wilhelmine shell of the Reichstag (1992-1999) was a given, even though it was Foster's job to exorcise the ghosts of its troubled past.

Each of these projects can be seen to provide clues for the Great Court; but each of them was also the product of a rather different set of circumstances. In Berlin the raw evidence of the past – Russian graffiti and vaults rudely deprived of their original mouldings – exists in sharp contrast to the new insertions. In the British Museum Foster has chosen a different strategy. While the walls of the courtyard and the interiors of the Reading Room are allowed to speak for themselves, everything else is determinedly new and finished with extreme precision. It is as if Foster is self-consciously expunging the humble, makeshift nature of the space as it was and dressing it to play the part of a national

Far left: Stonemasons cut a column drum for the new portico.

Left: Comparisons with Smirke's surviving stonework informed the design of the new masonry at every stage; here moulds are being taken of details on the East Portico.

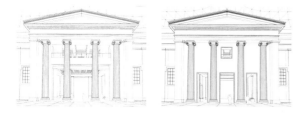

Left: At the time of the
competition the South Portico
was envisaged as an open
structure, with no walls between
the columns, which would have
created a sweeping spatial
continuum between the Front
Hall and the Great Court.
However, after consultation

with English Heritage, a more
traditional treatment was
adopted, in which the portico has
three defined openings (right).

institution. The decision to face the drum of the
Reading Room (a structure that was originally not
intended to be viewed externally and therefore had no
formal elevational treatment) with limestone, matching
the floor of the courtyard, has the effect of turning
the Great Court into a formal, unified space.

Encased in stone, and girdled by sweeping
staircases, the Reading Room stands at the centre of
the Great Court like a monumental obelisk, connected
only via the most tentative of glass links to Smirke's
Museum, to allow access from the existing upper-
level galleries. Everything else is kept deliberately
low-key.

Access to the rest of Foster's work at the museum
– the lower-level lecture theatres of the Clore
Education Centre and the facilities for school parties
in the Ford Centre for Young Visitors – is from pairs of
stairs sunk into unobtrusive openings pressed against
the south wall of the courtyard. To the north, in the
Wellcome Gallery, another pair of staircases leads
down to the Sainsbury African Galleries. Designed
as simple, flexible enclosures to allow the rotating
display of the collection, these five interlinked galleries
make it possible to appreciate the museum's fine
ethnographic holdings in the context of the other
great works in the collection.

As a visitor you are aware of the powerful presence
of the Great Court even before you reach it. The
meticulously restored Entrance Hall serves as a
prelude. Completed in the final phase of Sir Robert
Smirke's masterplan for the museum, in 1846, the
Entrance Hall was expanded in 1878 by the addition
of a third bay, which necessitated the demolition of
the South Portico. Foster has restored the space to
its original two-bay configuration, with direct access
into the Great Court via the rebuilt South Portico, and
faithfully reinstated the original decorative scheme.
Devised by Sydney Smirke and executed by Messrs
Collman & Davis, this scheme was historically
significant as the first major example in England of
a design based upon contemporary archaeological
excavations of Ancient Greek sites. The original carbon
arc light fittings have also been remade using working
drawings rediscovered in Germany.

Daylight leaks gently into the Entrance Hall from
the courtyard, urging you on across its floor until
you find yourself under that roof with its fascinating
optically dynamic structure, in the authoritative
presence of the Reading Room with its frieze of
inscribed lettering. Facing you is the doorway into the
Reading Room. The treatment of this doorway was
the subject of much debate within the Foster studio.

Right: The treatment of the
surprisingly small existing
doorway to the Reading Room
was the subject of much study.
The solution was to commission
Anish Kapoor to produce a
site-specific sculpture to stand
before the doorway as a marker.
It is seen here in model form.

Above: The roof in its final stages
of construction, seen during
spring 2000.

Left: The final glazed panel
is ceremoniously lowered
into place, 13 July 2000.

When it was built its height was limited by the position of the balcony structure within. Historically this had not been an architectural issue: the Reading Room had been reached via a low-ceilinged passageway. But in the changed context of the Great Court, it needed some form of articulation if it was not to look like a diminutive mouse hole in the wall. Foster looked at a variety of formal solutions, including a Classically detailed proposal, in keeping with the design for the portico, but eventually opted for a more contemporary idea: an unornamented doorway fronted by a sculptural marker. This led to the commissioning of Anish Kapoor to create a site-specific sculpture. (At the time of writing, this has not yet been installed.)

In its new guise as a library of 'world culture' the Reading Room plays a central role as the main information centre within the museum. It houses the Paul Hamlyn Library, a 25,000-volume public reference library for the study of world civilisations within the Walter and Leonore Annenberg Centre. This is both literally and metaphorically the hub of the museum. Here visitors can use the latest technology to access COMPASS, a database that allows a virtual tour of the museum's collections, or spend time in private study.

Within the Reading Room the familiar radial layout of tables has been retained and the furniture and

fittings restored. The original fresh-air ventilation system, in which grilles in the tables are served through the legs of a 'spider' of air ducts below the floor, has been reopened, while stale-air extract and smoke venting is through the new service void formed around the rotunda. The interior of the dome – which at 43 metres in diameter is some 9 metres greater than that of St Paul's Cathedral – has been restored to its original splendour and repainted in Sydney Smirke's azure, cream and gold decorative scheme. Using a system based on the maritime technique of 'caulking', which was used to seal the hulls of wooden ships, the dome's lining of papier mâché (a patented form of wood-pulp board) has been repaired using a flexible, bandage-like material called 'Flexiweave'. This will avoid future cracking caused by the movement of the cast-iron frame.

The completed project is an example of Foster's mature style, a highly accomplished, polished work of architecture, which has the effect of making a hugely complex and difficult project look simple to the point of inevitability; which is, of course, perhaps the most difficult of architectural tasks. But Foster's strategy for the Great Court can be explored at a number of levels.

First it addresses the urban issues. By sinking the necessary galleries and lecture theatres beneath the

Right: The lattice structure was
assembled from prefabricated,
ladder-like sections, which were
welded together on site.

Above left: An aerial view of the site in March 1999. The bookstacks have been cleared away and construction of the new courtyard floor is complete; work is progressing on the South Portico and the restoration of the existing stonework.

Above right: The site in January 2000; the roof structure is assembled, working from a temporary deck. Over a period of six months the ladder-like sections that made up the roof's structural steelwork were lifted on to the site by crane.

We wanted the roof structure to be visually as delicate and minimal as possible. We also wanted to allow the optimum amount of daylight into the Great Court, so creating the sensation of being in an outdoor space. Spencer de Grey, Foster + Partners, 2011

Above left: By February 2000 the roof structure was nearing completion and installation of the glazing had gathered pace, beginning above the North Portico and spreading out in a predetermined sequence to either side.

Above right: In April 2000 the roof glazing neared completion, although the temporary construction deck had not yet been removed.

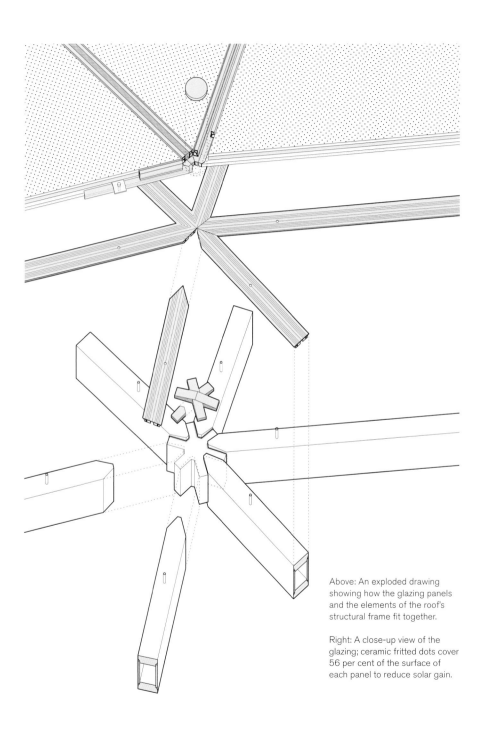

Above: An exploded drawing showing how the glazing panels and the elements of the roof's structural frame fit together.

Right: A close-up view of the glazing; ceramic fritted dots cover 56 per cent of the surface of each panel to reduce solar gain.

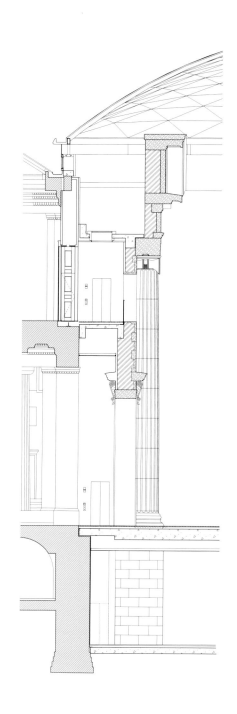
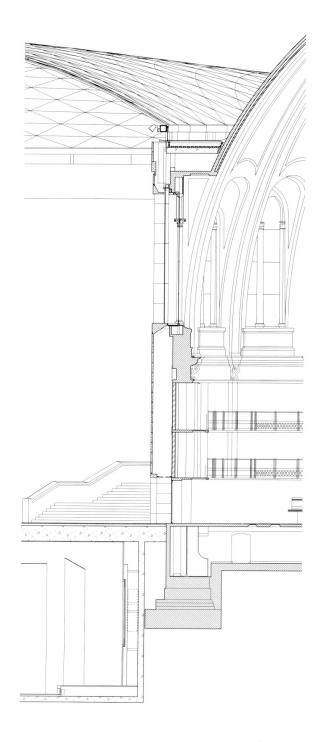

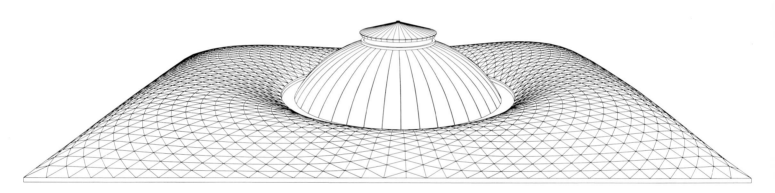

Opposite: Roof details at the perimeter of the Great Court, above the South Portico (left) and at the junction with the drum of the Reading Room. At the edge condition the roof sits on sliding bearings to allow differential movement between the steel structure and the masonry walls on which it bears.

Above: A drawing of the roof canopy in its final form, dating from January 1998. In total, the roof comprises 3,312 triangular glazed panels, no two of which are the same.

Overleaf: A plan of the museum, highlighting the new sequence of spaces created by the Great Court, and the corresponding aerial view.

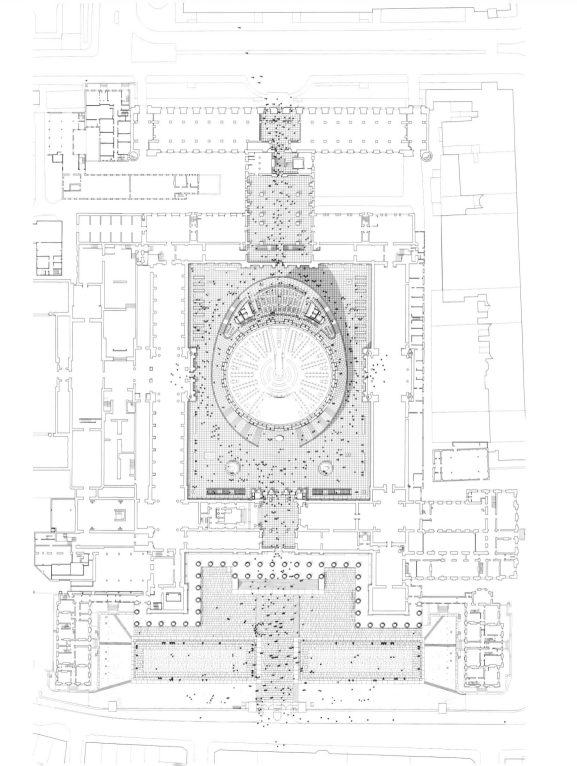

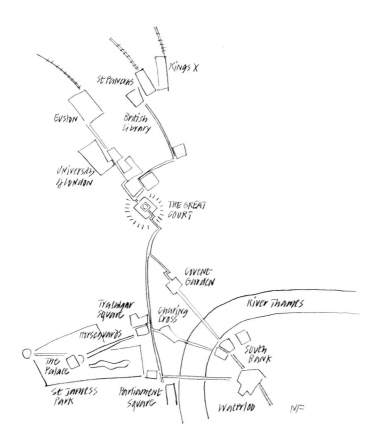

floor of the courtyard, Foster has freed the space of the courtyard itself and created a new principal level, corresponding with the main museum floor. Thus it has become a great urban space, conceived not just as the heart of the museum, but related to the city beyond. Visitors can now enjoy a sequence of spaces not so far removed from what Sir Robert Smirke originally intended. They move from the forecourt that he created facing Great Russell Street, through the museum's triumphal colonnade and the richly painted Entrance Hall into a sudden explosion of light and space beneath the billowing glass and steel roof. From there they may now continue, circulating around the drum of the Reading Room, and exiting the museum on the other side.

Secondly, Foster confronts the question of how to deal with such an important monument as the British Museum, and the extent to which historical authenticity is possible. The courtyard only existed in its original state for a brief period between 1847 and 1854, when construction of the library began. According to Panizzi's assistant – who cannot be considered entirely impartial – the courtyard was a 'dead loss'. Another critic called it the 'finest mason's yard in Europe'. And the public was excluded from what was by one account, 'a mere well of malaria, a pestilent congregation of vapours'.

Below: A sequence of images describing the new route created through the British Museum, experienced from north to south. From the North Entrance Hall, visitors pass through the Wellcome Gallery before entering the Great Court. From there, the route continues through the Front Hall, through the forecourt and out into Great Russell Street.

The courtyard was once symmetrical, with a portico in the centre of each facade (only the South Portico opened on to it, the others being 'blind'). But the southern portico was destroyed to extend the Entrance Hall in 1870. Together with the gradual destruction caused by the steady accretion of makeshift additions in the space over the years, the building also suffered bomb damage during the Second World War.

If you are rebuilding architecture with such a complex history, what do you do; how much do you restore? Smirke had wanted an open courtyard, so in the interests of authenticity, do you demolish the Reading Room? Clearly not. Do you restore the lost South Portico in the way it was actually built, or do you rebuild it as Smirke would have done, had he been given the money? Until 1833 Smirke had intended the facades in the quadrangle to carry elaborate porticoes, but budget cuts forced him to simplify them.

Foster and de Grey believed that for the Great Court to read as a coherent space, it was necessary to reconstruct the missing portico. It is not an exact replica, but a new design that reflects contemporary realities. As originally built, it had a domestically proportioned central door opening into the courtyard. A museum with six million visitors a year demanded something different. In their competition proposals

Foster and de Grey envisaged an open portico, with no walls between the columns. However, after consultation with English Heritage, who advocated a more conservative approach, they settled on three large doorways. The portico also stands further forward to accommodate new lifts and is pierced with an attic window – detailed with Foster's trademark glass balustrade – which provides a spectacular view out into the space that is anticipated in one of Smirke's surviving sketches. However, much critical comment has focused not on architectural detail, but on the precise origin of the stone that was used to build it. Instead of the Portland stone of the original, the stone used for the new portico was French, albeit from the same limestone bed that undulates deep beneath the English Channel.

Historical accuracy has always been a double-edged sword in the context of architectural restoration. William Morris established the Society for the Protection of Ancient Buildings to discourage the insensitive restoration of historical buildings, typified by the 'cathedral scrapers' of the nineteenth century. To Morris it was important not to diminish the integrity of the surviving genuinely ancient fragments of a building. Instead he advocated a strategy of patching and mending, of not pretending that new work was

from another period. In the British Museum it is unrealistic, and possibly even undesirable to expect an exact colour match between a stone that has spent many decades in the open air, and a later one that will always exist in a climate-controlled interior space.

Arguments about the authenticity of the stone, and the difference in colour between the new portico and the wall in which it is placed simply do not stack up. It is important to remember that the courtyard was not built in a single phase – it took almost twenty-five years to finish. Given the different length of exposure to the elements the colour of the stone around the courtyard would never have been entirely uniform, and it is not so now. It shows the wear and the scars of the passing of time.

Sooner or later, the stone episode will join the abundant supply of colourful tales that have always been part of the museum's history. The magnificent entrance front, for example, was built in the 1840s by Baker and Sons, a firm that had not submitted the lowest tender for the job, but which, according to Joseph Mordaunt Crook's riveting architectural history of the British Museum, had the vital qualification of a managing director married to the architect's sister.

The third, and perhaps most significant level of Foster's intervention is the degree to which the Great Court has fundamentally altered the way that visitors use the museum. Foster has reduced the pressure on the galleries, allowing people to experience the building not only as a series of galleries, but as a sequence of well-considered architectural spaces.

Above all, he has provided a sense of balance. The new spaces allow the museum to regain the dignity that they had lost under the pressure of the crowds of visitors. This is still a place that respects scholarship, even as it puts both Londoners and tourists at their ease. It balances history with the changing nature of the museum.

Learning from projects such as Nîmes, where the Carré d'Art has changed the fortunes of an entire quarter, the Great Court has transformed the social life of the British Museum. Even when the collections close for the night, the Great Court is designed to be alive with activity, as a place to socialise or join in the museum's continuing intellectual life. It is a covered version of an Italian square, full of people out for a stroll. You can have a meal or a glass of wine, or go to a lecture or a debate in the auditorium; or just spend a quiet moment under that extraordinary roof. It is the nearest that a museum can come to creating an authentic civic space.

Right: The forecourt seen after its restoration in 2000; the cars have gone and the forecourt is paved in York stone or gravelled in the less trafficked areas.

Above: Sir Robert Smirke's
original geometry for the
forecourt has been restored
and seating integrated into new
stone enclosures that surround
the grass parterres.

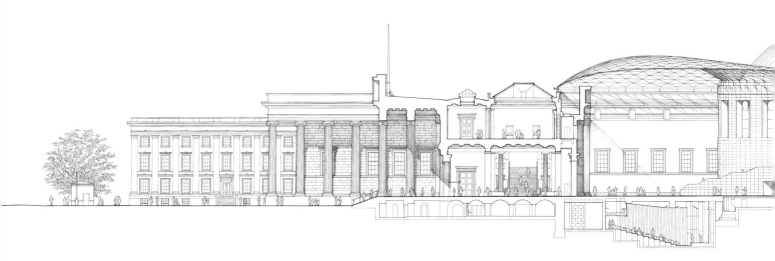

A cross-section along the
British Museum's north-south
axis, looking at the drum of
the Reading Room; within the
museum, the Great Court acts
as both a circulation hub and
a social focus.

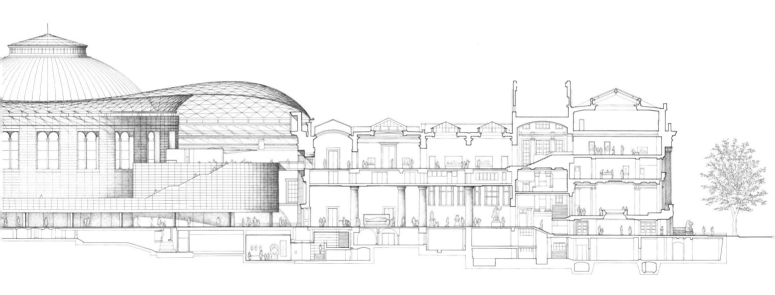

Above: The Front Hall and grand staircase were restored to their original polychromatic decorative schemes, devised by Sydney Smirke and executed by Messrs Collman & Davis in 1847.

Right: Looking from the restored Front Hall, through the South Portico into the Great Court.

At first the Great Court seems French in its spatial arrangement – formal, symmetrical, a straight-on axis from the entrance. But then you realise that it is more like an Italian urban space, in the way it pushes and pulls you in different directions. Paul Goldberger, *The New Yorker*, 8 January 2001

Following painstaking investigative
work, the colour and detail of the
Victorian decorative scheme in
the Front Hall was recreated using
traditional painting and gilding
techniques. The original scheme
was significant as the first
major example of polychromy in
England based on contemporary
archaeological excavations of
Ancient Greek sites.

Above: A quote from Alfred, Lord Tennyson's poem 'The Two Voices' is inscribed in slate in the Portland stone floor.

Right: Two staircases wrap around the drum of the Reading Room to take visitors to the restaurant and the Sir Joseph Hotung Gallery for temporary exhibitions on the upper levels.

Above: Looking into the Great
Court from the balcony of the
South Portico.

Right: The lantern is glimpsed
through one of the windows
of the round Reading Room.

Previous pages: The roof of the Great Court, seen in early morning sunlight.

Above and right: As the British Museum's social and physical hub, the Great Court has assumed some of the the character of a busy London square.

The space is bathed in light and there is a constantly changing, kaleidoscopic shadow play across the stonework from the tracery of the roof.

I marvelled at the roof's supple ability to soar through the air, and come to rest on top of Smirke's facades, without any visible means of support. Foster's mastery of minimal, elegant structures has never been more adroitly deployed. Richard Cork, *The Times*, 4 December 2000

Above: A glazed bridge provides a link between the restaurant terrace and the upper-level galleries in the North Wing.

Right: Looking up at the memorial inscription that lines the drum of the Reading Room.

The relationship between new and old is subtle; the Great Court is like a city square whose fabric has been altered and adapted over time.

Spiralling, tapering ribs chase each other round the vast space, scattering lattices of shadow on the flutes and volutes of the Ionic columns below.
Rowan Moore, *The Evening Standard*, 5 December 2000

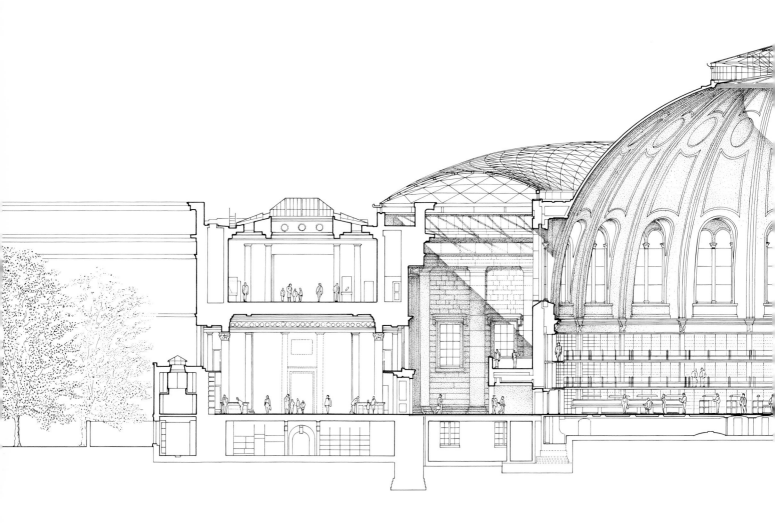

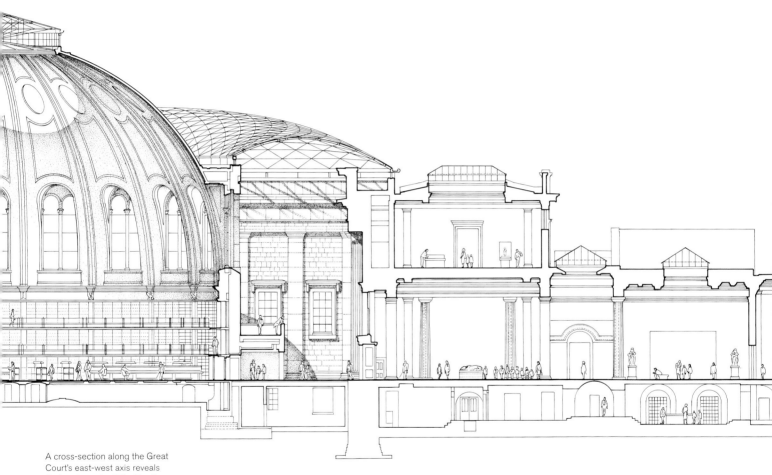

A cross-section along the Great Court's east-west axis reveals the heroic scale of the Reading Room when compared with the surrounding galleries and highlights the extent of the public space newly created within the museum.

Above and right: The Reading
Room plays a central role as
the museum's main information
centre and Library of World
Culture. Visitors can use the
latest technology to access
COMPASS, a database that
allows a virtual tour of the
museum's collections, or
spend time in quiet study.

Though the public space and roof provide the greatest thrill, the Reading Room is a close second. Its restoration is breathtaking. It allows visitors to rub shoulders with ghosts past and provides us all with a unique sense of place. Derek Walker, *Architecture Today*, February 2001

When the Reading Room opened it was described as '… a circular temple of marvellous dimensions, rich in blue and white and gold'. However, over time its colours disappeared beneath successive repaintings. It has been restored to Sydney Smirke's original decorative scheme – the first time it has been seen in living memory.

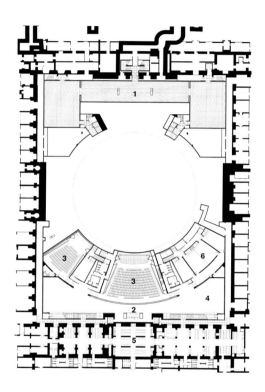

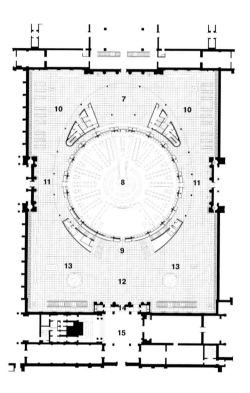

0   20m

0   60ft

Left: Plan at auditorium
level, immediately below
the Great Court.

Right: Plan at entrance level;
the floor of the Great Court
corresponds with the principal
level of the museum.

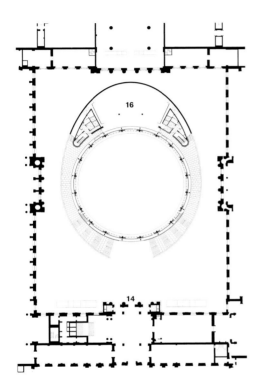

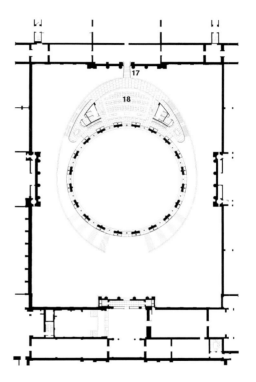

Left: Plan at the level of the
Sir Joseph Hotung Gallery.

Right: Plan at restaurant level.

1 Sainsbury African Galleries
2 Clore Education Centre
3 auditorium
4 conference foyer
5 Ford Centre for Young
   Visitors
6 seminar rooms
7 bookshop
8 Reading Room
9 entrance to Reading Room
10 services
11 retail
12 Great Court
13 information point
14 South Portico
15 Front Hall
16 Sir Joseph Hotung Gallery
17 bridge link to galleries
18 terrace restaurant

Above, right and overleaf: The Sainsbury African Galleries are located below the Great Court to the north of the Reading Room. These five interlinked rooms are designed as flexible enclosures to allow the display to be changed on a regular basis.

Above and right: With two cafés on the main level and a restaurant above, pausing for a coffee or enjoying a meal are among the Great Court's many pleasures.

The roof of the Great Court
captured at sunset.

If you could roam London as an aerial spirit you would be able to appreciate the glass canopy that, like a fin-de-siècle lampshade, sets the copper roof of the Reading Room as a jewel at the heart of the building. Eric Parry, *Architecture Today*, February 2001

Left and above: The Great Court is filled with activity throughout the day. An urban experience in microcosm the space encourages exploration and recreation. Its success as a social focus can be gauged by the ease with which visitors – especially schoolchildren – claim the space as their own.

Overleaf: An aerial view of the Great Court at night.

Facts and figures

Great Court at the British Museum

London, England
1994-2000

Client
Trustees of the British Museum

Project Team
Norman Foster
Spencer de Grey
Giles Robinson
Michael Jones

Julia Abell
William Castagna
Mark Costello
Daniel Goldberg
Nesa Marojevic
Peter Matcham
Filo Russo
Paul Simms
Pieter Vandendries
Oliver Wong
Diane Ziegler

Consultants
Structural, Mechanical and Electrical Engineer: Buro Happold
Planning Supervisor: Buro Happold
Acoustic Engineer: Sandy Brown Associates
Audio Visual: Mark Johnson Consultants
Construction Manager: Mace Ltd
Quantity Surveyors: Northcroft Nicholson/Davis Langdon & Everest
Facade Engineering: Emmer Pfenninger

Fire Engineering: FEDRA
Historic Buildings Advisor: Giles Quarme & Associates/Caroe & Partners/Ian Bristow
Lighting Designer: Claude Engle
Gallery Fit-out: British Museum Design Department
Gallery Lighting: George Sexton
Shop Fit-out: Carte Blanche
Signage: Baumann & Baumann
Catering: Digby Trout Restaurants/Tricon Foodservice Consultants

Principal Awards
2000/2001 National Heritage Museum of the Year Award
2001 Institute of Civil Engineers, Special Award
2002 Camden Design Awards
2002 Civic Trust Award
2003 RIBA Award
2003 ECCS European Steel Design Award
2003 The London Borough of Camden Building Quality Awards – Highly Commended
2006 Marble Architecture Award – Joint winner External Facings category

Project chronology

1993   November: Stage 1 of the architectural competition; 132 architects submit schemes
December: 22 architects are shortlisted by the selection panel

1994   March: Arup Associates, Rick Mather Architects and Foster + Partners are finalists
24 July: Foster + Partners are appointed as architects by the British Museum; Buro Happold are appointed as engineers and Davis Langdon & Everest as cost consultants

1995   The design is developed in discussion with the British Museum and English Heritage
December: a planning and listed building application is submitted to the London Borough of Camden

1996   The detailed design of the roof is refined; a system is developed that minimises the steelwork by integrating the main structural elements with the fixings and support for the glass

1997   January: the planning application is approved
Spring: Mace is appointed as construction manager to coordinate the many contractors for the project

During the course of the year, over three million books are removed from the British Library, including rare manuscripts

1998 2 March: demolition of the quadrant bookstacks begins
October: the majority of the bookstack buildings have been taken down to ground level, 3 metres (10 feet) lower than the surrounding galleries

1999 April: construction of the South Portico begins; individual stones weigh up to 7 tonnes
May: the northern half of the Great Court is enclosed by a temporary construction deck, allowing installation of the new roof structure to begin

2000 January: construction of the South Portico is completed
Spring: the structural lattice of the roof is completed and the majority of the glass has been installed; removal of the temporary scaffolding begins
13 February: a ceremony is held to mark the de-propping of the roof
13 July: the final glass panel in the roof is secured in position
6 December: the Great Court is officially opened by Her Majesty the Queen

Vital statistics

The Great Court is the largest covered public space in Europe

Project cost
£100 million; the project was supported by grants of £30 million from the Millennium Commission and £15.75 million from the Heritage Lottery Fund

Total project area
22,600 square metres

Total area of new facilities
13,990 square metres

Area of the inner courtyard
6,100 square metres

Weight of stone in the South Portico
1,500 tonnes

Largest piece of stone
8 tonnes

Area of restored courtyard stonework
6,000 square metres

Size of construction crane
46 metres high with a 75-metre jib (the longest in Europe) and a lifting capacity of 12 tonnes

The Reading Room
Reading Room ground floor area
1,350 square metres (approximately 21 per cent of the area of the courtyard)

Height from the floor to the apex of the dome
33 metres

Diameter of the dome
43 metres (exceeding the dome of St Paul's Cathedral, which measures 34 metres)

Diameter of the lantern
12 metres

Original dome lining
15mm of patent papier mâché

Materials used in the restoration
Cracks repaired with 2.4km of Flexiweave, a material similar to surgical bandage (sufficient to wrap 160 Egyptian mummies)
2 tonnes of paint was used
In excess of 12,000 books of 23.25 carat gold leaf were applied to recreate the original decorative scheme

The roof
Overall dimensions
96 metres by 72 metres

Overall area
6,100 square metres

Maximum distance spanned
40 metres

Minimum distance spanned
14 metres

Highest point above floor level
26.3 metres.

Steepest incline
52° to the horizontal

Shallowest incline
13° to the horizontal

Diameter of structural ring around
the Reading Room drum
    44 metres
Combined weight of glass and
steel elements
    800 tonnes
Weight of steel
    478 tonnes
Number of individual steel members
    5,162
Number of structural nodes
    1,826, each of which is unique with
    regard to x, y, and z coordinates
    and rotation angles
Steelwork tolerances
    Plus or minus 3mm
Number of glass panels
    3,312
Average panel area
    1.85 square metres
Panel geometry
    Smallest angle between the sides of
    one panel is 15°; the greatest is 30°
Total thickness of a glazing unit
    38.76mm
Double-glazed panel construction
    10mm body tinted, toughened glass
    outer layer; 16mm air cavity; inner
    layer of laminated glass comprising
    two panes of clear float glass and
    two clear PVB interlayers; white
    ceramic fritted dots are sealed into
    56 per cent of the inner surface of
    each panel to reduce solar gain

Environmental systems

Fresh air is brought into the space at
45 m3/second. Primary plant rooms in
the basement of the existing buildings
filter incoming air and full conditioning
is then undertaken by four secondary
plant rooms beneath the court

High-level louvres around the perimeter
of the Great Court provide natural
ventilation. These work in unison with
a direct fresh-air feed to recessed,
floor-level displacement louvres to allow
large stack effect and wind effect to
self-vent any internal heat gains

The Reading Room's original ventilation
system has been reinstated. A 'spider' of
brick air ducts beneath the floor supplies
air to outlet grilles in the tables

The glazing system, in which 56 per cent
of the surface of the glass is covered in
ceramic 'frits', prevents 75 per cent of
solar radiation penetration

An underfloor heating system is
achieved with a network of pipework
in the screed. The same pipework can
be fed from the chilled water system,
allowing the temperature in the Great
Court to be maintained between 18°C
in winter and 25°C in summer

The British Museum

1753   7 June: The British Museum is
        established by Act of Parliament;
        its holdings are largely based on
        the collections of the physician
        and scientist Sir Hans Sloane
        (1660-1753)
1759   15 January: The British Museum
        opens to the public in Montagu
        House in Bloomsbury, on the site
        of the current museum building
1802   In recognition of the increasing
        unsuitability of Montagu House,
        a Buildings Committee is
        established to plan the
        expansion of the museum
1816   The Elgin Marbles are
        transferred to the British
        Museum by Act of Parliament
1820   Architect to the Office of Works
        Sir Robert Smirke (1780-1867)
        is commissioned to design a
        new museum
1823   King George IV donates the
        personal library of King George
        III to the museum; it comprises
        60,000 volumes, 19,000
        pamphlets, maps, charts and
        topographical drawings
1823   Robert Smirke submits plans for
        a building surrounding a large
        central courtyard with a grand
        south front, to be constructed
        in phases

1827   The East Wing, built to house
       the King's Library opens; it is
       described as one of the finest
       rooms in London
1834   The north section of the West
       Wing, the Egyptian Galleries,
       is completed
1838   The North Wing housing the
       library and reading rooms
       is completed
1845   Sydney Smirke (1798-1877)
       succeeds his brother Robert as
       architect to the British Museum
1846   The West Wing and South Front
       are completed
1852   The opening of the forecourt
       marks the completion of Sir
       Robert Smirke's building
1853   The quadrangle building wins
       the Royal Institute of British
       Architects' Gold Medal
1857   The round Reading Room opens;
       designed by Sydney Smirke it is
       located in the museum's
       courtyard
1885   The White Wing, designed by
       Sir John Taylor (1833-1912),
       is completed
1895   The museum's trustees purchase
       69 houses surrounding the
       museum with the intention of
       demolishing them and building
       around the building's western,
       northern and eastern sides

1914   The King Edward VII Galleries,
       designed by Sir John Burnet
       (1859-1939), are completed
1938   The Duveen Gallery, designed by
       John Russell Pope (1874-1937)
       to house the Parthenon
       sculptures, is completed
1997   The British Library moves to its
       new building in St Pancras; until
       that point the British Museum
       was unique in housing a national
       museum of antiquities and a
       national library in the same
       building
2000   The Great Court is completed
2009   The British Museum celebrates
       its 250th anniversary; since it
       first opened to the public it is
       estimated that over 280 million
       people have visited the
       museum's unparalleled
       collection. The museum has
       almost 6 million visitors annually
       (5.93 million in 1998), making
       it the world's second most
       visited museum after the
       Louvre in Paris

Credits

Editor: David Jenkins
Design: Thomas Manss
& Company; Thomas Manss,
Tom Featherby
Picture Research: Gayle Mault,
Lauren Catten
Proofreading: Julia Dawson,
Rebecca Roke
Production Supervision:
Martin Lee
Reproduction: Dawkins Colour
Printed and bound in Italy
by Grafiche SiZ S.p.A.

The FSC®-certified paper
GardaMatt has been supplied
by Cartiere del Garda S.p.A., Italy

Picture credits

Photographs
Aerofilms: 45 (with additional
work by Gregory Gibbon)
British Museum: 35 (bottom left,
bottom right)
Richard Bryant/Arcaid: 27
(bottom left), 73
Richard Davies: 20, 21, 22 (top),
23 (top), 25
Foster + Partners: 15, 17, 24, 26,
31 (bottom left), 48 (top), 56, 57,
64-65
Ti Foster: 41
Dennis Gilbert/View: 18, 19 (top),
59
Hulton Archive: 16 (top, middle)
Timothy Hursley: 19 (bottom)
Ben Johnson: 60-61, 84-85,
94-95
National Monuments Record/
Warburg Institute: 16 (bottom)
Tim Soar: 62
Stanford University, Department
of Special Collections: 27 (top
left)
Nigel Young/Foster + Partners:
6-7, 31 (top left, top right, bottom
right), 32, 33, 34, 36, 37, 38, 39,
46, 47, 48 (bottom), 49, 52, 53,
54-55, 58, 63, 66, 67, 68-69, 72,
74-75, 78, 79, 80-81, 82, 83, 86,
87, 88-89

Drawings
Birds Portchmouth Russum:
50-51, 70-71
Buro Happold: 24 (bottom)
Norman Foster: 4, 5, 28-29, 46
(top)
Foster + Partners: 22 (bottom),
23, 24 (top), 26 (top), 35 (top),
42, 43, 44, 76, 77
Gregory Gibbon: 12-13
Birkin Haward: 27 (top right)
John Hewitt: 30, 40

Every effort has been made
to contact copyright holders.
The publishers apologise for
any omissions which they
will be pleased to rectify at
the earliest opportunity.

Editor's Note

In editing this book I am
particularly grateful to Norman
Foster and Deyan Sudjic for
their invaluable contributions.
I would also like to thank Thomas
Manss and Tom Featherby
for bringing the book to life
graphically; Gayle Mault and
Lauren Catten, who mined the
office archive; Julia Dawson and
Rebecca Roke for proofreading
the text; John Bodkin and Martin
Lee for overseeing production;
and the numerous people in the
Foster studio – past and present
– who helped piece together
the background to the project.

David Jenkins
London, August 2011